# Love Makes a Mess of Dying
## Greg Gilbert

smith|doorstop

Published 2019 by
Smith|Doorstop Books
The Poetry Business
Campo House
54 Campo Lane
Sheffield S1 2EG

Copyright © Greg Gilbert 2019
All Rights Reserved

ISBN 978-1-912196-20-3

Designed and Typeset by Utter
Printed by Biddles Books

**Acknowledgments**

With heartfelt gratitude to the following: Gillian Clarke, Carol Ann Duffy, Sasha Dugdale, Keiren Phelps, Stewart Foster and Dave Hubble.
Thanks also to Josephine Corcoran and Rishi Dastidar at *Andotherpoems* for sharing an extract from this sequence, and to Will Vigar for including my poetry in the anthology *Absent Ginsberg*.
To my family, whose love & support made these poems possible.
To Stacey Heale, whose strength and grace astounds me.

Smith|Doorstop Books are a member of Inpress: www.inpressbooks.co.uk. Distributed by NBN International, Airport Business Centre, 10 Thornbury Road Plymouth PL6 7PP

The Poetry Business gratefully acknowledges the support of Arts Council England.

# Contents

| | |
|---|---|
| 3 | Saturday, 1st August |
| 4 | Blue Draped Cube |
| 7 | Love Makes a Mess of Dying |
| 8 | On Your Thinking I Didn't Have Long |
| 9 | Reflection on Being the Singer in a Moderately Successful Indie Band Whilst Lying in Hospital |
| 10 | On Resignation |
| 11 | On Hope (A Partial Truth) |
| 12 | Discharged (And then alive, a shock to all, we headed out ...) |
| 13 | Seeing Winter as Death and Finding Solace |
| 14 | My Father the Conspiracy Theorist (Motivation From) |
| 15 | Settled Within |
| 17 | Holy River (Last Poem Written Before Diagnosis) |
| 19 | Brother |
| 20 | Creating an Image to Focus on During the First Bout of Chemotherapy |
| 21 | On Not Resembling Myself After Months Of Chemo & Comfort Eating |
| 22 | On Finding out about the Death of a Schoolmate After His Long Battle with a Brain Tumour |
| 23 | Scanxiety |
| 24 | The Sun is God |
| 26 | Overheard Couple in a Café / Café Life as Distraction |
| 27 | A Pact with God (One Year Since Prognosis) |
| 28 | 'Parent' is a Petrol-Blue Word |
| 29 | A Mouse's Wedding |
| 30 | Like Atlantis |
| 32 | Death Makes a Crown of Love |
| 33 | Tree Envy (The Field Again) |

*For Dalí and Bay*

## *Saturday, 1ˢᵗ August*

Graceful necks of wilting gold,
Dry grass sleeps upon the breeze;
My daughter's fine white hair,
Like cotton thread, lifts,
A cube of hissing morning
Bleeding through us.
In this field I invented summer
When I was cotton like her,
And from here all summers broke.

## *Blue Draped Cube*

The blue, the bed, the depth of it all, thick hospital drapes around us letting light under and over, fathoms deep, all breathless trepidation; who can I cling to? I cast around the blue space; the surgeon, the nurse, my dad and Stace are tucked up in the shadows, my Mother has absented herself, too raw and brittle from the past two weeks and believing herself bad luck. I've forgotten where my brother is.

The surgeon: "There's nothing to be done, I'm sorry," and I do think he's sorry but also embarrassed; eyes downcast, probably longing for the safety of the operating theatre, the nurse here to provide some pity which just pours from her brilliant blue eyes that, even in this fabric-dusk, shine like polished water.

I'm relieved when she shifts her attention to Stace, who sits down to my right, expression frozen in what I've termed in the past 'dust-bowl-farmer-wife-face', only now this face is laced with horror.

I've heard the surgeon's words but have retreated before truly comprehending them; telescoped back through my selves and into a new room that feels yellow and strung with tinnitus; from all the way back there I see my dad at the foot of the bed – angry, "For fucks sake!", helpless, rubbing his forehead, eyes absent and confused – and I can't begin to imagine what he is feeling and that sadness is the most real and compounds Stacey's horror and the nurse's piercing eyes with their practiced empathy and the surgeon's awkwardness and the words themselves, and all this choking, welling reality forces me out of the yellow room:

"How long have I got?"

And even as the words limp from my mouth I know they will exacerbate the pain – more for Stace, my dad – but I have to ask it because I don't think I can carry even a second more of not knowing, so I ask to relieve my own weight and I feel Stace buckle but feel myself engage with this new reality for the first time, making this sudden story almost a real thing, as if by not engaging it could've remained abstract, 'other' even – although the words felt strangely rehearsed and heavy – and as the surgeon shifts uncomfortably, face still kabuki, answering my own worn out question with another – "How long is a piece of string? Difficult to tell ..." – I feel the before-and-after-ness of this moment, a knot at the centre of my life from which all things stagger, the knot in my stomach that has drawn me like the rack. And all this is phasing in and out in snatches that stutter the surgeon's response still further and I find myself listening to the ward outside, so jealous of the other patients – beeping, wheezing, coughing, pained flirting with nurses – and I become aware of Stan in the bed to my left outside the blue cube who is throwing another of his fits, mean old bastard, railing at the nurses throughout the orange nights, not giving a fuck about the other sleepers, unabashed mien of the aged, something else to envy; I hear him bellowing "Don't touch my testicles!" (presumably the nurses are making another futile attempt at a bed-bath) and for a moment it seems painfully absurd, and for the same second I expect to see smirks on the gathered shady faces, spectral blues, everything in danger of collapse. But the shock holds sway.

And throughout my mother's absence grows heavier; no doubt she is pacing and fretting somewhere along the corridor, rehearsing all kinds of scenarios – I inherited her anxiety, we are twinned by it so I know ... the routine she's going through, a little dance, a little ritual to keep the bad at bay, I know all of this, how it spirals and encircles – and yet the reality is so much worse than she is imagining and someone has to tell her, God, this spectre is hanging over us. I probably feel how the surgeon felt coming here bearing life-shattering news, knowing it will drown expectant faces, my mother's face pulled and pale, but I know I won't have to deliver this news, my dad will; these are her last moments of not knowing.

At some point when there is nothing left to ask, when the empathy has been exhausted, the surgeon and nurse leave us and I thank him because he seemed so twitchy, out of place and awkward: I was ready for them to leave as soon as the surgeon had uttered "sorry".

Not long after, Dad leaves to find Mum and the time alone with Stace feels strikingly calm; something irrevocable has happened, carved up the world and moved on leaving us suspended.

"Life is wild" she says, our first words in this new reality.

We talk in quotes with hard edges, not really a conversation but an attempt to share truths quickly.

"I am so pleased you are here to hear this with me" – I mean this, adding "wherever I'm going, we're all going, we'll be together like space-ghosts."

"I will make sure our girls grow up unafraid" –'I' singular causes a lurching vertigo that sends me chasing my tail again: please don't plan ahead, don't past tense me, don't be used to this, I'm not ready to be used to this, to be as was, don't believe it because if you believe it I have to believe it and I can't believe it, don't make me other and expel me from us, step back, come back, I'll talk you back into the sanctuary of disbelief; all this hurtles across my head but the girls, Christ, through some primal cognitive dance I've managed to keep them out just to try to survive this moment, but now they suddenly loom, super-vivid and laughing – Dalí of the clouds and Bay all muddy and of the earth – and I'm nauseous to my bones.

"What have I done?"

The cube is lighter, the rhythms of the ward exacerbating the apprehension of facing my mother, which is taking far longer than anticipated – truly a waiting room – but she is coming with all the thunder of sleepless childhood nights, the school gates, the mud of football mornings, licking cake mix from the whisks, I've remembered where my brother is, here it comes, closing in, she enters the cube, I dissolve into her arms, her words "My boy, my boy," my words, "My girls, my girls."

## *Love Makes a Mess of Dying*

Love makes a mess of dying,
Requires a measure of healing
Between what you can allow yourself
And what you can allow others;

It holds you the centre
Of a tolerant universe; such
A simple thing for one, now splintered
Prismatic, unruly.

Love makes a mess of dying,
Rarefies what you've got left and
Draws close those for whom you've been
Essential architecture, each seeking
A totem.

Whatever tricks I tell myself to deaden before dying –
That I'm alone, that alone is the essential state – comes
Undone at the sight of love and I'm afraid, not of dying,
But of leaving a mess for love.

## *On Your Thinking I Didn't Have Long*

In my bones and gown,
You didn't think I'd make
Christmas, a murmuration
Of doubt scattered
At the surgeon's words

And I'm grateful you never said,
Let me bob with words devoid
Of knowing but light with care;
Yet I must've known at the point
Where our daughters met,

Where I know you utterly.
That your first thought was
David Lynch, that I might see
Twin Peaks before the end speaks

Of years and breath and simple,
Shared learning.

## *Reflection on Being the Singer in a Moderately Successful Indie Band Whilst Lying in Hospital*

I once sang on a mountainside,
My voice filling the air between flanks
And the sound of my shadow amplified,
Remade as a mountain.

Knowing my voice rang
Through villages like spring
Meant renewal of faith
In a bigger thing, happy
Not to understand. But this

Betrayal, the narrative upended
And suddenly failing beneath me;

It's all the contrast I can take, mountain
Lungs to melting lungs on these
Elevated pillows and the singer,
Whoever they are,
High and silenced.

## *On Resignation*

In the absence of a cure I choose
Abstinence; from feeling, from tender,
From signature, from footfall,
From astronomy, from tenses.
I choose to identify as non:
Non-believing,
Non-doubting,
Non-apparent.
Non- has no living so non- has
No dying.
Poverty of expression means I
Can only express as someone's I.
Non- has no I.

## *On Hope (A Partial Truth)*

The surgeon's truth is a partial truth,
The whole truth holds whatever science
May bring. When the oncologist
Invades the scene with shrewd calm
He sets me on a different tide:
Hope,
Small, to be cultivated with innocence.
With this grace the surgeon's words turn
Bitter from sour and I wonder
How he could've omitted
The only promise left to me.

Never having been hopeless, these
Hopeless days have been curious;
Matt and static, they
Crackle with an inverse height,
Flint and ringing.

But the oncologist only partially agrees
With the surgeon's words; he takes
The baton of my health and offers
A pinch of distance
Into which I can exhale:
Hope,
And, briefly, pain removes itself.

## *Discharged (And then alive, a shock to all, we headed out ...)*

By an open window mending slowly,
The hanging shade receding,
Hailing buds are flags of healing,
I find I sing an absent tune:
A slight invocation of waking pain
As preferable to distancing pain.

Awaiting visitors – daughters, my
Golden sovereigns, bubbling
Like mad honey – to pull me through
The window and into the sun
Torn with cobwebs from trees,
A press of seeds and wings;

By an open window listening
To the shifting plain of the day;
The morning was tall and thin
Like a tulip vase, afternoon is broad
Like an open casket
Letting all the birds in; a magpie
Drops to the fence like black ink
Through water, through sidewinding blossom,
And the coolness without passes within;

I'm a softening wax, a conductor's silence
Spreading like a picnic blanket
By an open window, captured.

## *Seeing Winter as Death and Finding Solace*

Each winter breath is a ghost
Of our recent selves:
We can learn to die easily,
No resistance just
A gentle shrug into everything.

No one mourns their breath in winter.
Though you watch the essence of you
Escaping. Winter has its reasons.

## *My Father the Conspiracy Theorist (Motivation From)*

My father the conspiracy theorist
Knows the history beneath history,
The news beneath news,
The meaning of words beneath words,

The Truth beneath Truth

And he knows I can beat this
And who am I to argue with Truth?

Oswald, an example of a man
With a mission, Ruby equally
So, see
        Anything is doable.

## Settled Within

I need to get my gods in order, they have grown unruly and I can't propitiate them all: when I was a kid I would confess every 'bloody' at the school gates, every blaspheme purged, but 'fuck' was a password to adolescence and my confessions abruptly ceased.

*Acutely alive to ritual, my family talked to ghosts and I listened closely:*

The summer blush of my Grandfather's skin told Romani descent, his Mother's burnt-owl stare out of the coal face past, transmitting her devilry like claws through sand: this pagan flourish passed like a flood and settled within.

Clergy would swell the shoebox of my Nan's sick room with their bruise-hued vestments like some prehistoric greenhouse, sipping tea whilst she, chastened with oxygen mask and pharoed with tissues, sputum cups and nebulizer, would mutely beam. My after-school by her side, Robert Powell's indecent eyes, settled within.

*I drew these stories like splinters from adults – the crystal ball kept in a black sock that only foretold woe; the maiden aunt as police oracle, on & on, etc, etc; drew these stories and they settled within as belief & compulsion.*

The reason I bring this up is because there was a point a few years back where I was so self-worn and pleading for hiding that I would picture life as a patient in hospital laid low with some manageable sickness, just ill enough to need tending. On occasion, this would be a light cancer, nothing insurmountable, but now I sometimes wonder if, through some spell of seeing, I made myself this. Look at the ego on me! You can't imagine the guilt, the regret, the wish for an inverse hex.

*(I feel cheated that, despite the cancer, I will never have an original thought about death. But, at the same time, an original thought about death might be too lonely to bear.)*


## *There Are No Secrets Here*

There are no secrets here, the ward looks through you.
But I wish to remain an invalid, an imposter:

I'm not sure I want to get well.

I don't want to be reasoned out of this bed.
The pain was the red of clenched eyelids – not blacking out
But narrowed and compressed into a livid strip
Of focused sensation; the anti-orgasm,
Nothing beyond the totality of it all.
My brain thinks getting well means going back to that
But in this bed, I don't have to parse and tease a presence.
Unaware of this, my relief is not my family's relief
And I wonder if they think I don't grasp the gravity of it all?

## *Holy River (Last Poem Written Before Diagnosis)*

The last of the ashes sink and we mind its writhing,
Witness its rhythmic dissolution amongst the oil and stick litter
As the filthy green swans draw near.

There are laws against this; the bank is silent, the houses indifferent,
Still we hide our tribute, simple geography: he
Fished here,

Against the bridge, its pocked and blistered iron
Played by sleepless engines, the crackling silver of river gills
Aping starlight overhanging.

This fact defines him. He was Santiago and thought me
His Manolin, the water, a giving thing, a
Sacred exchange.

We depart through the estate – orange, white and serpent coiled, –
A gift of years to the river, the swans with
Ashes on their feathers.

The applause of the swans at pace along the river
Breaks across the park, a thin, slow trajectory of
Patient heaving, a single wing between them,
Ashes on their feathers. Somewhere the silt chokes
A Roman road, at peace, visible maybe from height,
Binding lost Clausentum to the mudflats,
Where the houseboats suckle.

I catch their ascent above the terracotta,
Pulling for the porcelain white,
Their filthy green now playground grey
And I pull with them

(A wilful surge of the mind, to feel the fall of the earth
Beneath ecstatic flight, accompanying these seraphim
On their tour). And

All the noise of Solent airs hush upon us, fat vascular
Currents that gulp the traffic, the school bell, the church bell,
The dog scraps of gardens and parks,

A swallowing mass, the city, coins in the grass
Snug to the rusty Itchen; the Alps of refuse like a dragon's back
Heaving us on toward the docks

Where the cranes stitch the horizon,
And the old walls describe the city as was, the shore as was.
Our host bank

And the last of the ashes abandon their wings
And I fall with them, this agency of thought
Delivering us to the Tower, accepting us as loess.

Disentangled from limb and fate, we can let the salt blow through us,
On this sighted parapet,
Awaiting our next stirring.

## *Brother*

We overlap, that's the trouble my brother,
Little completions we each bring the other –
Our mother even dressed us the same
Despite our gulf in age – so to separate
Out this catastrophe is an impossibility
Because I know you must wear it
As a weight of support.


## *In Retrospect Our Love (What Cancer Has Given Us)*

In retrospect our love was prelude
To what this cancer has given us: a
Furious gaze through habit
To honest faces, a mirror
Of absolute clarity. Our doom together
Settled with a slamming finality, now
We can live in soundless colloquy
Like empty stones full of noiseless
Knowing.

*Creating an Image to Focus on During the First Bout of Chemotherapy*

And so, made resourceful
I create an image
For healing, to repel this
Poison's poison of vision
And aid a swift translation
From toxin to virtue:

A silver Cossack army
Wielding scimitars, the tumors
A petrified forest; the blades
Break on it as a chiming
Of flashing sickle moons, dense
As Mecca, sparks catching
The teeth of ecstatic horsemen.

My skin is false, but soon
The weather inside starts to tell
And my hair begins to fall
Like autumn, eyelashes
Land on my sketches.

*On Not Resembling Myself After Months Of*
*Chemo & Comfort Eating*

Sounding and looking like, at least
To myself, feels essential
Otherwise it's all too different.

One deep dark, sleepless
A figure loomed at me,
Broad – and for a moment
I quailed until I realised it
Was me in the long mirror,
Form so altered unfamiliar;

If the inside isn't me,
The exterior might recall –
Tell a surface tale of myself.
To remedy the loss.

## *On Finding out about the Death of a Schoolmate After His Long Battle with a Brain Tumour*

Particular blue arising
From the particular white of day
At evening; old skin thinning
To veins.

Didn't know you'd passed
As I noted the shade
Coming off the windows,
Assumed you'd be forever struggling,
On precipice but still on,
Ahead of our year, taking the
Flak arrows for life. The brave sun
In your face now online
In a hundred tributes and
We all shift a person closer,
The looming unbarred and the
Afterimage of your tears drawing

And evening kept going and became
Something else as you slipped
Off its back without me knowing.

*Scanxiety*

Let's say it's fatal, what do we do
With our days? Do we crack
The back of hours with every
Little thing, greedy for shared
Images, the one outgoing,
The other to carry and give
As eulogy? Or do we
Give our beings to each other,
The one to keep the other,
The both a gift to the bed, alloyed,
Urgent, bled?

Let's say it's inert and we have some
Leg room, a little allowance, do we
Let go of this shattering that has
Driven us further-quicker-deeper?
A sacrifice: we have aged outward
And these are new regions, as yet foreign.
If we let go of the catastrophe, we let go
Of this new country: do we cling to it?
And would that last? We are too
Small and stupid to know; through you
To landscape reaching, through me
To landscape pondering its next move.

## *The Sun is God*

Each lick of the wind on morning skin,
Branches staggered and awake
Like nerves to every degree
Of the earth's turn; window light
Affords blinding colour – the wince
Of a glorious morning – to eyes
Still precious & sore.

*'Intrude' is a word that gives the brain*
*The shape of its meaning: like arms*
*During breaststroke, it has an ease*
*To its invasion.*

Heat intrudes
On cold permanence:
Morning metals, calm and lifeless –
Cars are morning sculptures –
But soon warmth invades,
Evidence of a body,
Evidence we scratch
To retain despite sound proof
Of our being interlopers
In cold permanence.

Brief as dew, there are
Rivers that have never existed,
Oceans that have never sprung

For crossing. We fit where we're
Abandoned and intrusion happens
To everything eventually (right now, needles
Have triumphed over the skin).

Turner's dying words, 'The Sun Is God' – no:
Great cold nothing is the place in which
It all gathers, first and most powerfully.
If there is a God it is utterly blank
Potential and we must make
Peace with peace.

## *Overheard Couple in a Café / Café Life as Distraction*

If I sit back, the sun misses me
And hits the couple next to me,
Locked in doing life what you want –
Repeated, do what you want – and 'Cold Sweat'
Grinds against the window. The sun becomes
A molten finger through the window,
The couple next to me mention New York,
Vegas – change of faces; this is a moment
This a lever of life, why not if you have the talent
And skills – a dog-leg of being taking place
Whilst I sit back and let the sun miss me;
Living through dog-leg with hands over eyes –
It's a 'Family Affair' now no one can
Ever make you feel bad, the woman
Says little the man pours out such giving.
Thank you.

*A Pact with God (One Year Since Prognosis)*

One night, freshly home and
Toying with the fear, I made a pact
With God: give me ten years
To know my girls and do the things
I've not yet thought of and, for my part,
I'll try not to doubt.

But one year on a decade
Looks scant, single figures already
And barely happening. Was I too
Modest in my asking? Was there
A longer I limited? Do I beg
The same thing that allowed this thing
To stall this thing?

Nine years allotted no-evidence-of-
Listener but every evidence
Of illness, face upturned
Toward the plaster cracked
and gimlet fittings, I
Wish it a false start: start
Again, start again,
I wasn't ready.

# *'Parent' is a Petrol-Blue Word*

This morning we watched our daughter Dalí graduate from playschool, the children paraded before us wearing cardboard hats they'd made specially – shoddy windmills tipping and falling all over: utter momentary crystal, my head did that thing where I bookmark something as a poignant memory even as I'm living it. But amongst all these kids with their Mad Magazine faces, subdued for a spell at this intrusion of parents, I am never not aware of Dalí: she pulls at me like a dowsing rod and I can't help playing faces with her through the shoulders: expressions of slapstick confusion and each time she giggles I feel I have given.

*'Parent' is a petrol-blue word, both tense & in motion, but others might view it as orange & on the point of dissolve: it is vulnerable.*

I count the dads – it's a habit I've fallen into – hoping to offset the sore thumb of my presence: I count just two others.

I recognise I always understood my parents' burden: I seem to have always known that my dad's dad unexpectedly died in his arms – Francis after whom I'm named (or rather not according to the registrar, an oversight) – when my dad was 17. What do you do as a child when you know your parents have been wounded, too small to contain anything, to protect them, protect yourself, protect the egg of little time? The bright seasons of family, attempts to compensate for this tragedy, tragedy processed through gaiety with a gulf between easy for a child to fall into: deprived of another life that rumbled on elsewhere. And yet still I placed myself in front of speeding trains and walked window ledges, testing the remaining umbilical of care, a rite of terrible separation, always knowing I was wounding.

But this sickness, the Mother of all spite, what is this doing to them?

A glimpse is all I can manage, like sun-hurt snow too tender for touch.

# *A Mouse's Wedding*

We shall have a wedding so hidden
From emotion that it barely causes a ripple:
I half-joke it's a panic wedding and you half-laugh
And I half-wince to myself.

In sight of the ferries and their killing hulk,
Their carving of deep-cut beds, the fish
Unhoused, unmoored, we'll be wed; the
Bobbing craft nodding like Palm Sunday,
On to the island and its powdery cliffs
Which shrink like an aspirin (family
Holidays, ah, easy bliss – unknown to us,
We were all young then, even our parents,
Who I insist are still young though some
Are now dead. But they were here
Once, in the courtyard of the registry office,
Now lost and blown into the walls like Christmas
Laughter).

You and I will get married in August,
A mouse's wedding, no room for speeches.
Call it what it is: elegance, a way
To taper the messy ends of our shared
Lives. Over your shoulder, a past
Crouches like a fisherman with a harpoon,
But he is growing fainter and fainter
On the two tides that whip the island
To submission.

## *Like Atlantis*

It is real, isn't it? This bit of us & the sea?
It could easily be figment and I wouldn't
Be surprised: I often find myself living
As if the cancer were a fiction, a what-if
Tucked alongside England winning
The World Cup or Yellowstone Park
Erupting.

When I was last here I was so close
To death and didn't know it but photos
From that day preserve our complete denial
(One small wave could've snapped me,
My arms around the kids less than sand), now
A barely recognized season I feel
I once felt. But here we are again, briefly
Escaped & thicker set: the kissing coast
Adored by breakers that've rolled
From God knows where to land at our bare feet –
I don't remember the last time we were alone
With the sea and yet I can't say the thing
I need to say: "I don't want to die."

You can't give me what I need in return
And it would only make you feel helpless,
That's the selfish truth, and with our view
Set upon the sliding vastness it seems
A shame to shrink it to my life span.
Let's set this illness upon it
With our hurt: 18 months bruised

By 'living with it, not dying from it',
Only now knowing what that actually means:

*Not content to chew my gut it gnawed **us***
*Livid, it poisoned **us**, not until enemies but*
*Strangers.*

Let's picture it all now adrift on the glassy jade
and beg: smash it like Atlantis, will you?

A ceremony of care: we have no stone
Effigy but we do have the sea, the world's
Water thrown at us, and it's not hard
To imagine every ripple ever cast still living
Inside it, every voice lost upon it
Still reverberating below science,
Like some great warehouse of moment. Take
The prognosis, take the anguish, the comforting
Words, the arguments and desperation
And stash them deep and make them other
Whilst we reify our place, here, amongst
The living.

It is real, isn't it? This bit of us & the sea?
This, here, could be just three brushstrokes:
Sand, teal & cut cyanide.

## *Death Makes a Crown of Love*

Death makes a crown of love,
A mantle to take across the threshold
As a sign of accomplished living:
You are loved,
You have loved,
You have lived.

## *Tree Envy (The Field Again)*

Look at me in this field again,
You'd never guess there was a sky:
All suggestion and receding, the sun
Made peach by river mist,
The bare trees edgeless
And tissue-rent, I more so and fitting.

The ideation has been growing,
Not a plan you understand – I reassure
My therapist there are no plans –
But thoughts are a damp towel over
A chip-pan-fire, they suffocate
The spitting fat, but not the act –
I'm a coward and besides, love.

Not annihilation then, but I envy
The trees their shrouded morning
Where you wouldn't know them unless
You were at their feet. These limits
Make a realm in which I've shed so much –
The lip spit of kisses, the grease
Of burnt tyres and stolen engines.

At least one layer of this paling field
Is me and I watch me go without dying,
A forecast to behold and live: as the birds,
Bodiless, chorus this devour,
Its threshold – ash, fir and cow-parsley –
Slipping to milk with my eyes just
Articles in space.